T0302451

Celebrate Recovery®

Growing in Christ While Helping Others

The Journey Begins

PARTICIPANT'S GUIDE 4

John Baker is the founder of Celebrate Recovery®, a ministry started at Saddleback Church. It is estimated that over the last 25 years more than 1.5 million people have gone through this Christ-centered recovery program. There are currently over 27,000 churches that have weekly Celebrate Recovery meetings.

John has been on staff since Celebrate Recovery started. He has served as the Pastor of Membership, the Pastor of Ministries, and is currently the Pastor of Saddleback Church's Signature Ministries. He is also serving as one of the nine Elder Pastors at Saddleback. John is a nationally known speaker and trainer in helping churches start Celebrate Recovery ministries.

John's writing accomplishments include Celebrate Recovery's *The Journey Begins* Curriculum, *Life's Healing Choices*, the *Celebrate Recovery Study Bible* (general editor), and *The Landing* and *Celebration Place* (coauthor). John's newest books are *Your First Step to Celebrate Recovery* and *The Celebrate Recovery Devotional* (coauthor).

John and his wife Cheryl, the cofounder of Celebrate Recovery, have been married for more than four decades and have served together in Celebrate Recovery since the beginning. They have two adult children, Laura and Johnny, and five grandchildren.

Johnny Baker has been on staff at Celebrate Recovery since 2004 and has been the Pastor of Celebrate Recovery at Saddleback Church since 2012. As an adult child of an alcoholic who chose to become an alcoholic himself, Johnny is passionate about breaking the cycle of dysfunction in his family and helping other families find the tools that will lead to healing and openness. He knows that because of Jesus Christ, and by continuing to stay active in Celebrate Recovery, Maggie, Chloe, and Jimmy—his three children—will never see him drink. Johnny is a nationally recognized speaker, trainer, and teacher of Celebrate Recovery. He is a coauthor of the *Celebrate Recovery Daily Devotional*, *Celebration Place*, and *The Landing*, and is an associate editor of the *Celebrate Recovery Study Bible*. He has been married since 2000 to his wife Jeni, who serves alongside him in Celebrate Recovery.

REVISED EDITION

Celebrate Recovery®

Growing in Christ While Helping Others

PARTICIPANT'S GUIDE 4

The Journey Begins

A recovery program based on
eight principles from the Beatitudes

JOHN BAKER

FOREWORD BY RICK WARREN

ZONDERVAN®

ZONDERVAN

Growing in Christ While Helping Others

Requests for information should be addressed to:
Zondervan, *3900 Sparks Drive SE, Grand Rapids, Michigan 49546*

ISBN 978-0-310-13144-1 (softcover)
ISBN 978-0-310-13145-8 (ebook)

Interior design: Michelle Espinoza

Printed in the United States of America

Contents

Foreword by Rick Warren

You've undoubtedly heard the expression "Time heals all wounds." Unfortunately, it isn't true. As a pastor I frequently talk with people who are still carrying hurts from thirty or forty years ago. The truth is, time often makes things worse. Wounds that are left untended fester and spread infection throughout your entire body. Time only extends the pain if the problem isn't dealt with.

Celebrate Recovery® is a biblical and balanced program that can help you overcome your hurts, habits, and hang-ups. Based on the actual words of Jesus rather than psychological theory, this recovery program is more effective in helping people change than anything else I've seen or heard of. Over the years I've witnessed how the Holy Spirit has used this program to transform literally thousands of lives at Saddleback Church and help people grow toward full Christlike maturity.

Perhaps you are familiar with the classic 12-Step program of AA and other groups. While undoubtedly many lives have been helped through the 12 Steps, I've always been uncomfortable with that program's vagueness about the nature of God, the saving power of Jesus Christ, and the ministry of the Holy Spirit. So I began an intense study of the Scriptures to discover what God had to say about "recovery." To my amazement, I found the principles of recovery — in their logical order — given by Christ in His most famous message, the Sermon on the Mount.

My study resulted in a ten-week series of messages called "The Road to Recovery." During that series my associate pastor John Baker developed the four participant's guides, which became the heart of our Celebrate Recovery program.

As you work through these participant's guides, I trust that you will come to realize many benefits from this program. Most of all, however, my prayer for you is that, through Celebrate Recovery, you will find deep peace and lasting freedom in Jesus Christ as you walk your own road to recovery.

Dr. Rick Warren
Senior Pastor, Saddleback Church

Introduction

Congratulations! You have made it through the first six principles on your road to recovery. You began your journey by "Stepping Out of Denial into God's Grace." Then you faced the good and bad of your past by "Taking an Honest and Spiritual Inventory." And you just spent the last several months "Getting Right with God, Yourself, and Others."

Now you are ready to begin working on the last two principles along the road to recovery. These principles are much more than maintenance. As you practice them, they will help you continue "Growing in Christ While Helping Others," one day at a time!

Principle 7 is when you learn to take a daily INVENTORY and stand at the CROSSROADS of your recovery. You begin to live in newfound freedom in Christ. You learn that the best way to prevent a RELAPSE is to continue to grow in Christ through your quiet time and Bible study. In addition, Principle 7 will help you keep an "attitude of GRATITUDE."

And finally, in Principle 8 you understand how important it is to GIVE back to others what you have learned in your journey. Jesus will give you the courage to step out and say "YES" to helping newcomers and serving others.

In working with others, as sponsors or accountability partners, it is important for you to know the areas and reasons that can cause them to get stuck along their road to recovery. Lesson 25 includes the SEVEN REASONS WE GET STUCK IN OUR RECOVERIES.

After each lesson, there is an exercise for you to complete. Answer each question to the best of your ability. Don't worry about what you think the answer *should* be. Pray and then write down the answer from your heart. Remember John 8:32: "Then you will know the truth, and the truth will set you free."

After you have completed the exercise, share it with someone you trust. Your group, an accountability partner, or your sponsor (these are explained in Participant's Guide 2, Lesson 7) are all safe choices. You do not recover from your hurts, hang-ups, and habits by just attending recovery meetings. You must work and live the principles!

Now get ready for the rest of the journey that God has planned for you as you celebrate your recovery — one day at a time!

In His steps,
John Baker

The Road to Recovery

Eight Principles Based on the Beatitudes

By Pastor Rick Warren

1. **R**ealize I'm not God. I admit that I am powerless to control my tendency to do the wrong thing and that my life is unmanageable.
   "Happy are those who know they are spiritually poor."
   (Matthew 5:3)
2. **E**arnestly believe that God exists, that I matter to Him, and that He has the power to help me recover.
   "Happy are those who mourn, for they shall be comforted."
   (Matthew 5:4)
3. **C**onsciously choose to commit all my life and will to Christ's care and control.
   "Happy are the meek." (Matthew 5:5)
4. **O**penly examine and confess my faults to myself, to God, and to someone I trust.
   "Happy are the pure in heart." (Matthew 5:8)
5. **V**oluntarily submit to every change God wants to make in my life and humbly ask Him to remove my character defects.
   "Happy are those whose greatest desire is to do what God requires."
   (Matthew 5:6)
6. **E**valuate all my relationships. Offer forgiveness to those who have hurt me and make amends for harm I've done to others, except when to do so would harm them or others.
   "Happy are the merciful." (Matthew 5:7)
   "Happy are the peacemakers." (Matthew 5:9)
7. **R**eserve a daily time with God for self-examination, Bible reading, and prayer in order to know God and His will for my life and to gain the power to follow His will.
8. **Y**ield myself to God to be used to bring this Good News to others, both by my example and by my words.
   "Happy are those who are persecuted because they do what God requires." (Matthew 5:10)

Twelve Steps and Their Biblical Comparisons*

1. We admitted we were powerless over our addictions and compulsive behaviors, that our lives had become unmanageable.

   "For I know that good itself does not dwell in me, that is, in my sinful nature. For I have the desire to do what is good, but I cannot carry it out." (Romans 7:18)

2. We came to believe that a power greater than ourselves could restore us to sanity.

   "For it is God who works in you to will and to act in order to fulfill his good purpose." (Philippians 2:13)

3. We made a decision to turn our lives and our wills over to the care of God.

   "Therefore, I urge you, brothers and sisters, in view of God's mercy, to offer your bodies as a living sacrifice, holy and pleasing to God — this is your true and proper worship." (Romans 12:1)

4. We made a searching and fearless moral inventory of ourselves.

   "Let us examine our ways and test them, and let us return to the LORD." (Lamentations 3:40)

5. We admitted to God, to ourselves, and to another human being the exact nature of our wrongs.

   "Therefore confess your sins to each other and pray for each other so that you may be healed." (James 5:16)

6. We were entirely ready to have God remove all these defects of character.

   "Humble yourselves before the Lord, and he will lift you up." (James 4:10)

7. We humbly asked Him to remove all our shortcomings.

"If we confess our sins, he is faithful and just and will forgive us our sins and purify us from all unrighteousness." (1 John 1:9)

8. We made a list of all persons we had harmed and became willing to make amends to them all.

"Do to others as you would have them do to you." (Luke 6:31)

9. We made direct amends to such people whenever possible, except when to do so would injure them or others.

"Therefore, if you are offering your gift at the altar and there remember that your brother or sister has something against you, leave your gift there in front of the altar. First go and be reconciled to them; then come and offer your gift." (Matthew 5:23 – 24)

10. We continued to take personal inventory and when we were wrong, promptly admitted it.

"So, if you think you are standing firm, be careful that you don't fall!" (1 Corinthians 10:12)

11. We sought through prayer and meditation to improve our conscious contact with God, praying only for knowledge of His will for us and power to carry that out.

"Let the message of Christ dwell among you richly." (Colossians 3:16)

12. Having had a spiritual experience as the result of these steps, we try to carry this message to others and to practice these principles in all our affairs.

"Brothers and sisters, if someone is caught in a sin, you who live by the Spirit should restore that person gently. But watch yourselves, or you also may be tempted." (Galatians 6:1)

* Throughout this material, you will notice several references to the Christ-centered 12 Steps. Our prayer is that Celebrate Recovery will create a bridge to the millions of people who are familiar with the secular 12 Steps (I acknowledge the use of some material from the 12 Suggested Steps of Alcoholics Anonymous) and in so doing, introduce them to the one and only true Higher Power, Jesus Christ. Once they begin that relationship, asking Christ into their hearts as Lord and Savior, true healing and recovery can begin!

Serenity Prayer

If you have attended secular recovery programs, you have seen the first four lines of the "Prayer for Serenity." The following is the complete prayer. I encourage you to pray it daily as you work through the principles!

Prayer for Serenity

God, grant me the serenity
to accept the things I cannot change,
the courage to change the things I can,
and the wisdom to know the difference.
Living one day at a time,
enjoying one moment at a time ;
accepting hardship as a pathway to peace ;
taking, as Jesus did,
this sinful world as it is,
not as I would have it ;
trusting that You will make all things right
if I surrender to Your will ;
so that I may be reasonably happy in this life
and supremely happy with You forever in the next.
Amen.

Reinhold Niebuhr

Celebrate Recovery's Small Group Guidelines

The following five guidelines will ensure that your small group is a safe place. They need to be read at the beginning of every meeting.

1. Keep your sharing focused on your own thoughts and feelings. Limit your sharing to three to five minutes.
2. There is NO cross talk. Cross talk is when two individuals engage in conversation excluding all others. Each person is free to express his or her feelings without interruptions.
3. We are here to support one another, not "fix" another.
4. Anonymity and confidentiality are basic requirements. What is shared in the group stays in the group. The only exception is when someone threatens to injure themselves or others.
5. Offensive language has no place in a Christ-centered recovery group.

Lesson 19

Crossroads

Principle 7: Reserve a daily time with God for self-examination, Bible reading, and prayer in order to know God and His will for my life and to gain the power to follow His will.

Step 10: We continued to take personal inventory, and when we were wrong, promptly admitted it.

"So, if you think you are standing firm, be careful that you don't fall!" (1 Corinthians 10:12)

Think About It

Jesus says, "If you live as I tell you to, . . . you will know the truth, and the truth will set you free" (John 8:32, TLB). By working the principles and following Christ's directions, the foundation of your life has been rebuilt. You will undoubtedly see major changes in your life, if you haven't already! But now you are at the CROSSROADS of your recovery.

First Corinthians 10:12 warns us, "So, if you think you are standing firm, be careful that you don't fall!" Steps 10 through 12 (Principles 7 and 8) are where we will live out our recoveries for the rest of our time here on earth. They are much more than maintenance steps, as some have referred to them. These are the "how I want to live the rest of my life steps and principles."

As we begin to work Step 10[1], we will see that it is made up of three key parts, each one corresponding to the acrostic for this lesson, TEN.

1. Please note that though Step 10 and Principle 7 differ somewhat in their focus, both point toward the same result: the character and image of Christ in our daily life. This chapter will emphasize the step more than the principle, but in no way do we intend to discount the many benefits of daily living Principle 7.

Take time to do a daily inventory

1. The *what* : "We continued to take personal inventory . . ."

"Let us examine our ways and test them, and let us return to the LORD." (Lamentations 3:40)

Evaluate the good and the bad parts of our day

2. The *why*: " . . . and when we were wrong . . ."

"If we say that we have no sins, we are only fooling ourselves, and refusing to accept the truth . . . we are lying and calling God a liar, for he says we have sinned." (1 John 1:8 – 10, TLB)

Need to admit our wrongs promptly

3. The *then what*: " . . . promptly admitted it."

"This is how I want you to conduct yourself in these matters. If you enter your place of worship and, about to make an offering, you suddenly remember a grudge a friend has against you, abandon your offering, leave immediately, go to this friend and make things right. Then and only then, come back and work things out with God." (Matthew 5:23 – 24, MSG)

Practice keeping a daily journal for one week. Write out your daily inventory — the good and the bad. Look for negative patterns, issues that you are repeatedly writing down and having to promptly make amends for! Share them with your sponsor or accountability partner, and set up an action plan for you — with God's help and power — to overcome them.

Write About It

1. Before you start working on Step 10, take a moment to reflect and list some of the changes in your life that have come from working the steps and principles with Jesus as your Higher Power.

   - How has your behavior changed?

   - What specific relationships have been restored or improved?

   - How has your relationship with Jesus grown since you began your journey of recovery?

   - List the new relationships that you have made along your journey.

2. In your own words, what does Step 10 mean to you?

    - The *what*: "We continued to take a personal inventory . . ."

    - The *why*: " . . . and when we were wrong . . ."

    - The *then what*: " . . . promptly admitted it."

3. Keep a daily journal over the next seven days. Record the good along with the bad. Write down victories and areas of needed growth. Look for patterns. Share them with your sponsor or accountability partner at the end of the week.

Your Step 10 Journal

Day One

Day Two

Day Three

Day Four

Day Five

Day Six

Day Seven

4. What did you learn by keeping your journal?

5. What areas did you identify as strengths?

6. What areas do you need to work on?

Suggestion: It's a Healthy Habit!

Keeping a daily journal is a key tool to help you stay on track on your road to recovery. You've done it for seven days, why stop now?

Daily Inventory

Principle 7: Reserve a daily time with God for self-examination, Bible reading, and prayer in order to know God and His will for my life and to gain the power to follow His will.

Step 10: We continued to take personal inventory and when we were wrong, promptly admitted it.

"So, if you think you are standing firm, be careful that you don't fall!" (1 Corinthians 10:12)

Think About It

In Principle 7 and Step 10, we begin to apply what we have discovered in the first six principles and nine steps: We humbly live in reality, not denial; we have done our best to make amends for our past; we desire to grow daily in our new relationships with Jesus Christ and others.

God has provided us with a daily checklist for our new lifestyle. It's called the "Great Commandment":

"'Love the Lord your God with all your heart . . . soul and . . . mind.' This is the first and greatest commandment. And the second is like it: 'Love your neighbor as yourself.' All the Law and the Prophets hang on these two commandments." (Matthew 22:37 – 40)

James 1:22 encourages us: "Do not merely listen to the word, and so deceive yourselves. Do what it says." When we practice the Great

Commandment, we become doers of God's Word, living examples of Christ. Our walk lines up with our talk! The apostle Paul lived that way. He says in 1 Thessalonians 1:5 (TLB), "Our very lives were further proof to you of the truth of our message."

There are three ways to do a Step 10 inventory.

Ongoing

We can do this periodically throughout the day. The best time to admit we are wrong is the exact time that we are made aware of it! Why wait? We need to make amends ASAP! We will sleep a lot better at night!

Daily

At the end of each day we need to look over our daily activities — the good and the bad. We need to search for where we might have harmed someone or where we acted out of anger or fear. The best way to do this is to keep a journal! Then the next morning as promptly as we can, we need to admit mistakes and make our amends.

Periodic

Every three months, get away for a "mini retreat." Bring your daily journal with you. Pray and read your daily entries. Ask God to show you areas in your life that you can improve over the next ninety days and the victories that you have made in the last ninety days!

The Bible gives us instructions on how to avoid the necessity of making an amends in Step 10:

"Intelligent people think before they speak; what they say is then more persuasive." (Proverbs 16:23, GNT)

"Let no foul or polluting language, nor evil word nor unwholesome or worthless talk (ever) come out of your mouth, but only such (speech) as is good and beneficial to the spiritual progress of others." (Ephesians 4:29, AB)

"A wise, mature person is known for his understanding. The more pleasant his words, the more persuasive he is." (Proverbs 16:21, GNT)

"A word of encouragement does wonders!" (Proverbs 12:25, TLB)

"If I had a gift of being able to speak in other languages without learning them, and could speak in every language there is in all of heaven and earth, but didn't love others, I would only be making noise." (1 Corinthians 13:1, TLB)

Step 10 daily action plan

1. Continue to take a daily inventory, and when you are wrong, promptly make your amends.
2. Summarize the events of your day in your journal.
3. Read and memorize one of the Step 10 verses (see above).
4. Work all steps and principles to the best of your ability.

The key verse for this lesson is Mark 14:38: "Watch and pray so that you will not fall into temptation. The spirit is willing, but the flesh is weak."

Principle 7a Prayer

Dear God, thank You for today. Thank You for giving me the tools to work my program and live my life differently, centered in Your will. Lord, help me to make my amends promptly and ask for forgiveness. In all my relationships today help me to do my part in making them healthy and growing. In Jesus' name I pray, Amen.

Write About It

1. What are some of the advantages of each of the three types of inventories in your recovery? How can they help you to "be careful that you don't fall"?

- Ongoing:

- Daily:

- Periodic (monthly, quarterly, or annually):

2. What do the following verses mean to you and how can they help you in this step?

   "From a wise mind comes careful and persuasive speech." (Proverbs 16:23, TLB)

   "Don't use bad language. Say only what is good and helpful to those you are talking to, and what will give them a blessing." (Ephesians 4:29, TLB)

"The wise man is known by his common sense, and a pleasant teacher is the best." (Proverbs 16:21, TLB)

"Anxious hearts are very heavy but a word of encouragement does wonders!" (Proverbs 12:25, TLB)

"If I had a gift of being able to speak in other languages without learning them, and could speak in every language there is in all of heaven and earth, but didn't love others, I would only be making noise." (1 Corinthians 13:1, TLB)

"Watch with me and pray lest the Tempter overpower you. For though the spirit is willing enough, the body is weak." (Mark 14:38, TLB)

3. What is your daily action plan for Step 10?

4. What are the recurring events or issues that you are constantly needing to make amends for?

   - With your family?

   - With your friends?

   - With those you work with?

   - With those in your church or recovery program?

Principle 7a Verses

"As God's messenger I give each of you God's warning: Be honest in your estimate of yourselves, measuring your value by how much faith God has given you." (Romans 12:3, TLB)

"Cling tightly to your faith in Christ and always keep your conscience clear, doing what you know is right." (1 Timothy 1:19, TLB)

"Cross-examine me, O Lord, and see that this is so; test my motives and affections too." (Psalm 26:2, TLB)

"We can justify our every deed but God looks at our motives." (Proverbs 21:2, TLB)

"A sensible man watches for problems ahead and prepares to meet them. The simpleton never looks, and suffers the consequences." (Proverbs 27:12, TLB)

"Keep a close watch on all you do and think. Stay true to what is right and God will bless you and use you to help others." (1 Timothy 4:16, TLB)

"So be careful. If you are thinking, 'Oh, I would never behave like that' — let this be a warning to you. For you too may fall into sin." (1 Corinthians 10:12, TLB)

"Come to terms quickly with your enemy before it is too late." (Matthew 5:25, TLB)

"My brothers and sisters, when you have many kinds of troubles, you should be full of joy, because you know that these troubles test your faith, and this will give you patience." (James 1:2 – 3, NCV)

"A relaxed attitude lengthens a man's life; jealousy rots it away." (Proverbs 14:30, TLB)

Lesson 21

RELAPSE

Principle 7: Reserve a daily time with God for self-examination, Bible reading, and prayer in order to know God and His will for my life and to gain the power to follow His will.

Step 11: We sought through prayer and meditation to improve our conscious contact with God, praying only for knowledge of His will for us and power to carry that out.

"Let the message of Christ dwell among you richly." (Colossians 3:16)

Think About It

The best ways to prevent relapse can be summarized in the acrostic RELAPSE.

Reserve a daily quiet time

Principle 7 sums it up best: Reserve a daily time with God for self-examination, Bible reading, and prayer in order to know God and His will for my life and *gain the power* to follow His will.

> *"Watch and pray so that you will not fall into temptation. The spirit is willing, but the flesh is weak." (Mark 14:38)*

Evaluate

Your evaluation needs to include your physical, emotional, relational, and spiritual health. And don't forget the value of doing a "H-E-A-R-T" check. Are you

Hurting
Exhausted
Angry
Resentful
Tense

Special instructions for this step are found in Romans 12:3 – 17 (TLB): "Be honest in your estimate of yourselves. . . . Hate what is wrong. Stand on the side of the good. Love each other. . . . Be patient in trouble. . . . Do things in such a way that everyone can see you are honest clear through."

Listen to Jesus

We need to take a time-out from the world's "rat race" long enough to listen to our bodies, our minds, and our souls. We need to slow down enough to hear the Lord's directions.

"Test everything that is said to be sure it is true, and if it is, then accept it." (1 Thessalonians 5:21, TLB)

"Let everyone be sure that he is doing his very best, for then he will have the personal satisfaction of work well done and won't need to compare himself with someone else." (Galatians 6:4, TLB)

"Listen to the Lord. Hear what he is telling you." (Isaiah 1:10, TLB)

Alone and quiet time

Jesus Christ spent time alone with His Father. You need to do the same. Set a daily appointment time to be alone with God. Listen carefully; learn how to hear God!

"Be still, and know that I am God." (Psalm 46:10)

Plug into God's power through prayer

God's guidance and direction can start when your demands stop! Be specific in your prayer requests; pray about everything, asking for God's perfect will.

"Don't worry about anything; instead, pray about everything; tell God your needs and don't forget to thank him for his answers." (Philippians 4:6, TLB)

Slow down long enough to hear God's answer

We can become impatient. We want our prayers answered now! We need to remember that our timing can be flawed, while God's timing is perfect!

"Listen to me. Keep silence and I will teach you wisdom!" (Job 33:33, TLB)

"If you do this you will experience God's peace, which is far more wonderful than the human mind can understand. His peace will keep your thoughts and your hearts quiet and at rest as you trust in Christ Jesus." (Philippians 4:7, TLB)

Enjoy your growth

Rejoice and celebrate the small successes along your road to recovery! Always remember you're on a journey, a journey of several steps. Maintaining an "attitude of gratitude" is like taking spiritual vitamins.

Share your victories — no matter how small — with others in your group. Your growth will give others hope!

"Be joyful always, pray at all times, be thankful in all circumstances. This is what God wants from you in your life in union with Christ Jesus" (1 Thessalonians 5:16, GNT)

Here are a few final suggestions for preventing relapse:

1. Pray and read your Bible daily. Establish a specific time of day to have your "quiet time."
2. Make attending your recovery meeting a priority. Stay close to your support team.

3. Spend time with your family (if they are safe). If they are not, spend time with your church family.
4. Get involved in service. Volunteer!

Write About It

1. What are some of the ways (tools) that you have developed in your recovery to prevent relapse?

2. Do a **H-E-A-R-T** check right now. Are you

   Hurting?

   Exhausted?

   Angry?

   Resentful?

   Tense?

3. Specifically, what do you do when you are

   Hurting?

   Exhausted?

   Angry?

   Resentful?

   Tense?

4. Rate your listening skills from 1 to 10, 10 being the best.

   - What are some ways that you think you could improve your listening skills with others?

   - What are some ways that you could improve your listening skills with God?

5. Describe what a "quiet time" means to you and why it is important.

6. How could you improve your prayer time? Be specific.

   When do you pray?

   Where do you pray?

7. After you pray, do you slow down long enough to hear God's answer? What does the word "meditation" in this step mean to you?

8. What are some of the other things that you do in your recovery to help you on your journey and prevent relapse?

9. I think we all agree that recovery is a joy, but it also requires hard work. What do you do to celebrate your recovery — even the small victories?

Gratitude

Principle 7: Reserve a daily time with God for self-examination, Bible reading, and prayer in order to know God and His will for my life and to gain the power to follow His will.

Step 11: We sought through prayer and meditation to improve our conscious contact with God, praying only for knowledge of His will for us and power to carry that out.

"Let the message of Christ dwell among you richly." (Colossians 3:16)

Think About It

One of the greatest ways to work Principle 7 and to prevent relapse is to maintain an "attitude of gratitude."

In your prayers this week focus on your gratitude toward GOD, OTHERS He has placed in your life, your RECOVERY, and your CHURCH.

Be thankful to God

"Do not be anxious about anything, but in every situation, by prayer and petition, with thanksgiving, present your requests to God." (Philippians 4:6)

"Let us give thanks to the LORD for his unfailing love and wonderful deeds for mankind." (Psalm 107:15)

Be thankful for others

"Let the peace of Christ keep you in tune with each other, in step with each other. None of this going off and doing your own thing. And cultivate thankfulness. Let the word of Christ — the Message — have the run of the house." (Colossians 3:15 – 16, MSG)

Be thankful for your recovery

"As for us, we have this large crowd of witnesses around us. So then, let us rid ourselves of everything that gets in the way, and of the sin which holds on to us so tightly, and let us run with determination the race that lies before us." (Hebrews 12:1, GNT)

Be thankful for your church

"Enter the Temple gates with thanksgiving." (Psalm 100:4, GNT)

Principle 7b Prayer

Dear God, help me set aside all the hassles and noise of the world to focus and listen just to You for the next few minutes. Help me get to know You better. Help me to better understand Your plan, Your purpose for my life. Father, help me live within today, seeking Your will and living this day as You would have me.

It is my prayer to have others see me as Yours; not just in my words but, more importantly, in my actions. Thank You for Your love, Your grace, Your perfect forgiveness. Thank you for all those You have placed in my life, for my program, my recovery, and my church family. Your will be done, not mine. In Your Son's name I pray, Amen.

Write About It

1. Why do you think it is important for you to maintain an "attitude of gratitude" in your recovery?

2. In what three areas of your recovery are you especially thankful for God's power? Try to think of areas of growth or positive change in you that only God could have accomplished.

   a.

   b.

   c.

3. Name three people God has placed in your recovery who you are grateful for and why.

   a.

   b.

   c.

4. What three areas of your recovery ministry, small groups, or other events are you thankful for? Why?

    a.

    b.

    c.

5. List three things that you are thankful for in your church. Be specific.

    a.

    b.

    c.

6. Congratulations! You have just completed your first *gratitude list.* Review it. How does it make you feel?

7. Let the individuals on your list know what an impact they have had on your recovery, and thank each of them personally!

Principle 7b Verses

"The whole Bible was given to us by inspiration from God and is useful to teach us what is true and to make us realize what is wrong in our lives; it straightens us out and helps us do what is right."
(2 Timothy 3:16, TLB)

"Now your attitudes and thoughts must all be constantly changing for the better."
(Ephesians 4:23, TLB)

"Be still, and know that I am God." (Psalm 46:10)

"Job, listen to this: Stop and notice God's miracles."
(Job 37:14, NCV)

"And if you leave God's paths and go astray, you will hear a Voice behind you say, 'No, this is the way; walk here.' "
(Isaiah 30:21, TLB)

"Oh, the joys of those who do not follow evil men's advice, who do not hang around with sinners, scoffing at the things of God. But they delight in doing everything God wants them to, and day and night are always meditating on his laws and thinking about ways to follow him more closely."
(Psalm 1:1 – 2, TLB)

"So now you can look forward soberly and intelligently to more of God's kindness to you when Jesus Christ returns. Obey God because you are his children; don't slip back into your old ways — doing evil because you knew no better." (1 Peter 1:13 – 14, TLB)

"Watch your step. Stick to the path and be safe. Don't sidetrack; pull back your foot from danger." (Proverbs 4:26 – 27, TLB)

"Watch with me and pray lest the Tempter overpower you. For though the spirit is willing enough, the body is weak."
(Mark 14:38, TLB)

"Be glad for all God is planning for you. Be patient in trouble, and prayerful always."
(Romans 12:12, TLB)

"You are living a brand new kind of life that is continually learning more and more of what is right, and trying constantly to be more and more like Christ who created this new life within you."
(Colossians 3:10, TLB)

"If you want to know what God wants you to do, ask him, and he will gladly tell you, for he is always ready to give a bountiful supply of wisdom to all who ask him; he will not resent it."
(James 1:5, TLB)

Lesson 23

GIVE

Principle 8: Yield myself to God to be used to bring this Good News to others, both by my example and by my words.

"Happy are those who are persecuted because they do what God requires." (Matthew 5:10)

Step 12: Having had a spiritual experience as the result of these steps, we try to carry this message to others, and practice these principles in all our affairs.

"Brothers and sisters, if someone is caught in a sin, you who live by the Spirit should restore that person gently. But watch yourselves, or you also may be tempted." (Galatians 6:1)

Think About It

"Freely you have received; freely give." (Matthew 10:8)

What does it mean to GIVE?

God first

By placing God first in your life, you will realize that everything you have is a gift from Him. You realize that your recovery is not dependent on material things. It is built upon your faith and your desire to follow Jesus Christ's direction.

"[He] did not even keep back his own Son, but offered him for us all! He gave us his Son — will he not also freely give us all things?" (Romans 8:32, GNT)

"You cannot serve two masters: God and money. For you will hate one and love the other, or else the other way around." (Matthew 6:24, TLB)

I becomes we

The 12 Steps do not begin with the word "I." The first word in Step 1 is "we." The road to recovery is not meant to be traveled alone.

"'Love the Lord your God with all your heart and with all your soul and with all your mind.' This is the first and greatest commandment. And the second is like it: 'Love your neighbor as yourself.'" (Matthew 22:37 – 39)

"Two are better off than one, because together they can work more effectively. If one of them falls down, the other can help him up. But if someone is alone . . . there is no one to help him. . . . Two people can resist an attack that would defeat one person alone." (Ecclesiastes 4:9 – 12, GNT)

Victories shared

God never wastes a hurt! Principle 8 gives us the opportunity to share our experience and victories. "This is how it was for me. . . ." "This is what happened to me. . . ." "This is how I gained the strength. . . ." "There's hope for you."

"Let us give thanks to the God and Father of our Lord Jesus Christ, the merciful Father, the God from whom all help comes! He helps us in all our troubles, so that we are able to help those who have all kinds of troubles, using the same help that we ourselves have received from God." (2 Corinthians 1:3, GNB)

Example of your actions

In James 1:22 it says we are to be "doers of the word." But to be of help to another, we are to "carry the message in all our affairs."

You have all heard the term "Sunday Christians." Let us not become just "Friday night recovery buffs."

"My children, our love should not be just words and talk; it must be true love, which shows itself in action." (1 John 3:18, GNT)

The Lord spreads His message through the eight principles and the Christ-centered 12 Steps. We are the instruments for delivering the Good News. The way we live will confirm to others the sincerity of our commitment to our Lord, to the program, and to them! That's Principle 8.

"No one lights a lamp and then covers it with a washtub or shoves it under the bed. No, you set it up on a lamp stand so those who enter the room can see their way. . . . We're not hiding things; we're bringing everything out into the open. So be careful that you don't become misers. . . . Generosity begets generosity. Stinginess impoverishes." (Luke 8:16 – 18, MSG)

Write About It

1. What does Matthew 10:8 — "Freely you have received; freely give" — mean to you?

2. How has your attempt to put God first in your life changed your understanding of the word "give"?

3. Ecclesiastes 4:9 tells us that "two are better than one." List specific instances in your own recovery that you have seen this verse in action.

4. What are some of your recent victories that you could share with a newcomer?

5. In James 1:22 we are told to be "doers of the Word." How can you be a doer of the Word

   - among family and friends?

- in your recovery group?

- in your church?

- on the job?

- in your community?

Lesson 24

YES

Principle 8: Yield myself to God to be used to bring this Good News to others, both by my example and by my words.

"Happy are those who are persecuted because they do what God requires." (Matthew 5:10)

Step 12: Having had a spiritual experience as the result of these steps, we try to carry this message to others and to practice these principles in all our affairs.

"Brothers and sisters, if someone is caught in a sin, you who live by the Spirit should restore that person gently. But watch yourselves, or you also may be tempted." (Galatians 6:1)

Think About It

When you reach this step you are ready to say YES to service.

Yield myself to God

Principle 8 sums up the *Y*: Yield myself to God to be used to bring this Good News to others, both by my example and by my words.

"If a Christian is overcome by some sin, . . . humbly help him back onto the right path, remembering that the next time it might be one of you who is in the wrong. Share each other's troubles and problems, and so obey our Lord's command." (Galatians 6:1 – 2, TLB)

Example is what is important

Your walk needs to match your talk because your lifestyle reflects what you believe. Does your lifestyle show others the patterns of the world — selfishness, pride, and lust — or does it reflect the love, humility, and service of Jesus Christ?

"Arouse the love that comes from a pure heart, a clear conscience, and a genuine faith." (1 Timothy 1:5, GNT)

"Let us not love with words or tongue but with actions and in truth." (1 John 3:18)

Serve others as Jesus Christ did

When you have reached Principle 8, you are ready to pick up the "Lord's towel," the one with which He washed the disciples' feet in the upper room.

"And since I, the Lord and Teacher, have washed your feet, you ought to wash each other's feet. I have given you an example to follow: do as I have done to you." (John 13:14 – 15, TLB)

How You Can Say YES

1. *Be an accountability partner.* Look for someone in your small group who will agree to encourage and support you as you work through the principles. You agree to do the same for that person. You hold one another accountable for working an honest program.

2. *Be a sponsor.* Sponsors are people who have worked the principles or the steps. Their job is to guide newcomers on their journey through the program, to give a gentle nudge when they are procrastinating or slow them down when they are rushing through a step. Sponsors do so by sharing their personal journey on their road to recovery.

3. *Be involved in Celebrate Recovery and your church.* There are many opportunities for service in this recovery ministry and in your church.

You have come to the fork in your road to recovery.

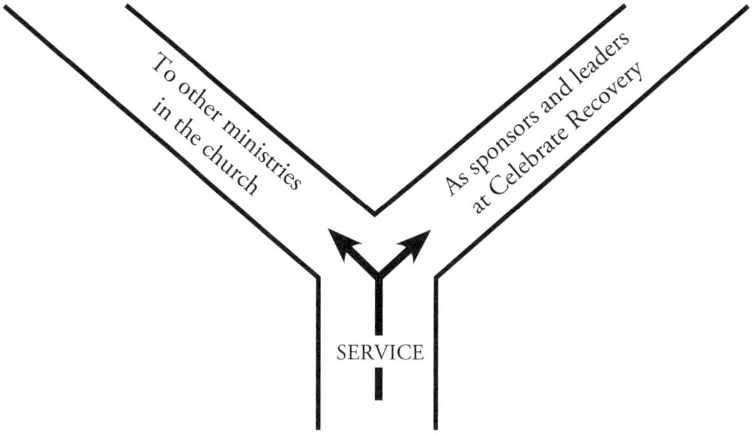

Remember, "You can't keep it unless you give it away!"

Principle 8 Prayer

Dear Jesus, as it would please You, bring me someone today whom I can serve. Amen.

Write About It!

1. If you knew that you couldn't fail, what would you like to do most for God in helping others?

2. What are some ways you can pick up the Lord's towel (John 13:14 – 15) today and start serving others?

3. What does the illustration of the fork in your road to recovery say to you?

4. In the words of Step 12, how will you "practice these principles in all [y]our affairs"?

5. Describe what the phrase "You can't keep it unless you give it away" means in your recovery.

6. Create your own action plan for Principle 8.

   I am going to explore opportunities to serve in the following areas:

   a.

   b.

   c.

Principle 8 Verses

"What a wonderful God we have — he is the Father of our Lord Jesus Christ, the source of every mercy, and the one who so wonderfully comforts and strengthens us in our hardships and trials. And why does he do this? So that when others are troubled, needing our sympathy and encouragement, we can pass on to them this same help and comfort God has given us." (2 Corinthians 1:3 – 4, TLB)

"But watch out! Be very careful never to forget what you have seen God doing for you. May his miracles have a deep and permanent effect upon your lives! Tell your children and your grandchildren about the glorious miracles he did." (Deuteronomy 4:9, TLB)

"In the same way, faith by itself, if it is not accompanied by action, is dead." (James 2:17)

"Live and act in a way worthy of those who have been chosen for such wonderful blessings as these." (Ephesians 4:1, TLB)

"But we Christians have no veil over our faces; we can be mirrors that brightly reflect the glory of the Lord." (2 Corinthians 3:18, TLB)

"In response to all he has done for us, let us outdo each other in being helpful and kind to each other and in doing good." (Hebrews 10:24, TLB)

"When God's children are in need, you be the one to help them out. . . . Don't just pretend that you love others; really love them. Hate what is wrong. Stand on the side of the good." (Romans 12:13, 9, TLB)

"Dear brothers, if a Christian is overcome by some sin, you who are godly should gently and humbly help him back onto the right path, remembering that next time it might be one of you who is in the wrong." (Galatians 6:1, TLB)

"Two can accomplish more than twice as much as one, for the results can be much better. If one falls, the other pulls him up; but if a man falls when he is alone, he's in trouble. . . . And one standing alone can be attacked and defeated, but two can stand back-to-back and conquer; three is even better, for a triple-braided cord is not easily broken." (Ecclesiastes 4:9 – 12, TLB)

Lesson 25

Seven Reasons We Get Stuck

As you complete your journey, you will discover the rewards of sponsoring newcomers. Your role as a sponsor will be to help others along their journey on the road to recovery by guiding them through the principles and steps. Your task is not to pick them up and carry them through the steps, but to stand alongside them as they complete their journey.

At times, you may need to slow them down when they are moving through the steps too quickly; or you may need to speed them up when they get stuck along the side of the road. There are seven major areas in which I have seen individuals get "stuck" at some point in their recoveries. It is important that you are familiar with each of them so you help them get "unstuck."

You have not completely worked the previous principle

Perhaps you are trying to move through the principles too quickly. Slow down! Give God time to work! Remember, this program is a process.

"Since we live by the Spirit, let us keep in step with the Spirit."
(Galatians 5:25)

You have not completely surrendered your life and your will to the Lord

Perhaps you are trusting Jesus with the "big" things, but you still think you can handle the "small" things.

"For good judgment and common sense, trust in the Lord completely; don't ever trust in yourself. In everything you do, put God first, and he will direct you and crown your efforts with success." (Proverbs 3:5 – 6, TLB)

You have not accepted Jesus' work on the cross for your forgiveness

You may have forgiven others, but you think your sin is too big to be forgiven.

"But if we confess our sins to him, he can be depended on to forgive us . . . from every wrong." (1 John 1:9, TLB)

"So overflowing is his kindness towards us that he took away all our sins through the blood of his Son, by whom we are saved." (Ephesians 1:7, TLB)

Have you forgiven yourself?
Remember,

"Therefore, there is now no condemnation for those who are in Christ Jesus." (Romans 8:1)

You really have not forgiven others who have harmed you

You must "let go" of the pain of past harm and abuse. Until you are able to release it, forgive it, it will continue to hold you as its prisoner.

"After you have suffered a little while, our God, who is full of kindness through Christ, will give you his eternal glory. He personally will pick you up, and set you firmly in place and make you stronger than ever." (1 Peter 5:10 – 11, TLB)

You are afraid of the risk in making the necessary change

You may be paralyzed by the fear of failure. You may fear intimacy because of the fear of rejection or of being hurt again. You may resist change (growth) because of the fear of the unknown.

*"Fear not, for I am with you. Do not be dismayed. . . .
I will strengthen you; I will help you; I will uphold you
with my victorious right hand." (Isaiah 41:10, TLB)*

*"That is why we can say without any doubt or fear,
'The Lord is my Helper and I am not afraid of anything
that mere man can do to me.' " (Hebrews 13:6, TLB)*

You are not willing to "own" your responsibility

You need to take responsibility for your past in a broken relationship, a damaged friendship, with a distant child or parent, and so forth.

*"Examine me, O God, and know my mind; test me, and discover
. . . if there is any evil in me and guide me in the everlasting way."
(Psalm 139:23, GNT)*

You have not developed an effective support team

Do you have a sponsor or an accountability partner? Do you have the phone numbers of others in your small group? Have you volunteered for a commitment to your recovery ministry?

*"Be with wise men and become wise. Be with evil men
and become evil." (Proverbs 13:20, TLB)*

*"Dear brothers, you have been given freedom: not freedom
to do wrong, but freedom to love and serve each another."
(Galatians 5:13, TLB)*

*"Share each other's troubles and problems, and so obey
our Lord's command." (Galatians 6:2, TLB)*

Afterword

CONGRATULATIONS! You have completed all eight principles and all 12 Steps! I do not have to tell you that was not an easy accomplishment! There are many rewards found in this Christ-centered program. It is important that you share your "miracle" with others. You are a living example of God's grace. I pray for your continued growth in Christ, your recovery, and your service to others. Below please find Celebrate Recovery's Daily Action Plan for Serenity.

In His steps,
John Baker

Celebrate Recovery's Daily Action Plan for Serenity

1. Daily, continue to take an inventory. When you are wrong, promptly admit it.
2. Daily, study God's Word and pray asking God to guide you and help you apply His teaching and will in your life.
3. Daily, work and live the eight principles to the best of your ability, always looking for new opportunities to help and serve others — not just at your recovery meetings but in all areas of your life.